CHRISTMAS COOKIES

THE CHRISTMAS TREASURY

CHRISTMAS COOKIES

NELSON REGENCY
A Division of Thomas Nelson, Inc.

A THOMAS NELSON BOOK

First published in 1993 by
Thomas Nelson Publishers, Nashville, Tennessee.

Copyright © 1993 by
Michael Friedman Publishing Group, Inc.

10 9 8 7 6 5 4 3 2 1

Library of Congress Cataloguing in Publication Data is available.

Library of Congress Card
92-084144

ISBN 0-8407-6915-6

THE CHRISTMAS TREASURY:
CHRISTMAS COOKIES
was prepared and produced by
Michael Friedman Publishing Group, Inc.
15 West 26th Street, New York, N.Y. 10010

Editor: Kelly Matthews
Art Director: Jeff Batzli
Designer: Robert W. Kosturko
Photography Editor: Daniella Jo Nilva

Printed in Hong Kong and bound in China

METRIC CONVERSION CHART

For your convenience, we suggest that you use the following table for adapting to metric measurement. The table gives approximate, rather than exact, conversions.

SPOONS

1/4 teaspoon	= 1 milliliter
1/2 teaspoon	= 2 milliliters
1 teaspoon	= 5 milliliters
1 tablespoon	= 15 milliliters
2 tablespoons	= 25 milliliters
3 tablespoons	= 50 milliliters

CUPS

1/4 cup	= 50 milliliters
1/3 cup	= 75 milliliters
1/2 cup	= 125 milliliters
2/3 cup	= 150 milliliters
3/4 cup	= 175 milliliters
1 cup	= 250 milliliters
1 pint	= 500 milliliters
1 quart	= .95 liters
1 gallon	= 3.8 liters

TO ADAPT LENGTHS

one inch = 2.5 centimeters
one foot = 30 centimeters
one yard = .9 meters

OVEN TEMPERATURES

200°F	= 100°C
225°F	= 110°C
250°F	= 120°C
275°F	= 140°C
300°F	= 150°C
325°F	= 160°C
350°F	= 180°C
375°F	= 190°C
400°F	= 200°C
425°F	= 220°C
450°F	= 230°C
475°F	= 240°C

TO ADAPT WEIGHTS

one ounce = 28 grams
one pound = .45 kilograms

CONTENTS

Introduction

THERE IS PERHAPS NO BETTER WAY TO BRING THE SPIRIT OF THE Christmas season into your home than by preparing homemade cookies. The delicious fragrance of cookies baking in the oven is indeed a signal that the holiday season has begun. Baking Christmas cookies is both enjoyable and relaxing, and it is an activity that can be even more fun and memorable when shared with a friend or with children. Children love to help bake cookies, and oftentimes, they can even make their very own.

Homemade cookies also make perfect Christmas presents. They make personal, thoughtful gifts, because they are made with tender, loving care and are given from the heart. Rather than buying another gift-wrapped package from the department store, why not show how much you care by spending your time and talent creating something special. And people of all ages are certain to enjoy your special gift. It's hard to think of anyone who doesn't like homemade cookies. In addition, don't forget that cookies are very easy and inexpensive to make, benefits that any gift-giver is bound to appreciate.

There are also many beautiful ways to gift-wrap cookies. You can easily arrange them in one of the many attractive boxes and tins available at gift and craft shops. Or if you feel more creative, take a container that is already in the house, such as an empty coffee can or nut tin, wrap it with decorative paper, and embellish it with a festive ribbon. Cookies also look wonderful placed in an attractive basket and then wrapped with special, colorful see-through plastic wrapping paper.

If you plan to send cookies through the mail, there are a few things to keep in mind. Cookies should always be placed in layers that are separated by tissue paper, waxed paper, or foil. Moist cookies should be separated from crispy cookies, and strongly flavored cookies should be contained in their own airtight wrappings so that their flavor won't be absorbed. Always pack the cookies snugly, filling extra space with tissue paper, and be sure to ship them in a sturdy cardboard box. And last of all, do take time to sit back, relax, and enjoy that special plate of cookies you reserved for yourself!

FRUITCAKE SQUARES

Fruitcake squares take a traditional Christmas dessert and turn it into something new and fun. These chewy, goody-filled cookies can withstand a long voyage and are perfect to ship to friends and loved ones far away.

1 cup all-purpose flour
¼ teaspoon salt
½ teaspoon baking soda
½ teaspoon ground cinnamon
½ cup butter, softened
¾ cup granulated sugar
2 eggs
8 ounces pitted dates, chopped
¼ cup mixed candied fruit

½ cup red candied cherries, quartered
¾ cup chopped nuts
Red and green candied cherries, reserved for garnish

FROSTING
1½ cups confectioners' sugar
2½ tablespoons milk, more if necessary

Preheat oven to 375°F. Grease and flour a 13" x 9" x 2" pan. In a small bowl, blend flour with salt, soda, and cinnamon. In a large bowl, beat butter, sugar, and eggs at medium speed until light and fluffy. Stir in flour mixture, dates, candied fruits, quartered cherries, and nuts. Spread in prepared pan and bake 30 minutes until golden.

In the meantime, prepare the frosting by mixing together the confectioners' sugar and milk. Stir until smooth, and then cover with a damp cloth until ready to use. Wait until cake has cooled, and cut into 2" x 1" bars. Then frost, using a butter knife or spatula, and decorate with red and green candied cherries. Store, wrapped in waxed paper, in a covered tin.

YIELD: 4 dozen squares

GERMAN FRUITY SPRITZES

COLORED JAMS MAKE THESE SPRITZ BARS GLISTEN LIKE stained glass. They can also be made with jam tinted red and green to brighten any gift box or cookie tray with the traditional Christmas colors.

- 1 cup butter, softened
- ½ cup brown sugar, packed
- 1 egg
- 1 teaspoon vanilla
- 2¼ cups flour

- 1 teaspoon baking powder
- 2 cups raspberry, strawberry, or pineapple jam (can be tinted red or green)

Cream together the butter and brown sugar, then add the egg and vanilla. Sift the flour and baking powder together, and then gradually stir them into the creamed ingredients until smoothly incorporated.

Put half the dough into a cookie press with a 1-inch ribbon plate. Press out 10 strips, each 10 inches long, onto ungreased baking sheets. Now change the plate to a star decorators' tip, and using the rest of the dough, form a rim along the sides of each of the 10 ribbons. The dough rim should be piped on top of the existing dough. Carefully spoon jam down the centers of the strips.

Bake at 400°F for 8 to 10 minutes. While cookies are still hot, cut strips on the diagonal 1¼ inches wide, then let cool.

YIELD: 4 dozen

Pecan Triangles

Like the best pecan pies, these cookies are sweet and rich, with a pleasing nutty flavor. Cut them into triangles and pop them into your mouth.

1⅓ cups all-purpose flour
½ cup plus 2 tablespoons brown sugar, packed
½ cup butter, softened
2 eggs
½ cup light corn syrup

1 cup chopped pecans
2 tablespoons butter, melted
1 teaspoon vanilla
¼ teaspoon salt
Confectioners' sugar

Preheat oven to 350°F, and grease a 9-inch-square baking pan. In a small bowl, mix flour and the 2 tablespoons brown sugar. Work in ½ cup butter with fingers until dough begins to hold together. Press onto bottom of greased pan. Bake 12 to 15 minutes. Cool.

In medium bowl, beat the ½ cup brown sugar and eggs until light and fluffy. Beat in corn syrup, pecans, melted butter, vanilla, and salt. Pour on crust. Bake 25 minutes or until edges are lightly browned. Cool for 2 hours.

Sprinkle cake with confectioners' sugar. Cut into 3-inch squares. Cut each square in half to make a triangle.

YIELD: 18 triangles

PENNSYLVANIA DUTCH ALMOND COOKIES

COOKIES ARE A CENTRAL PART OF THE CHRISTMAS CUSTOMS of the Pennsylvania Dutch. This is just one of the many cookies they make for the holidays.

1 cup butter
1 cup confectioners' sugar
4 egg yolks
3 tablespoons cream
3 cups sifted flour

ICING
2 egg yolks
2 tablespoons water
Confectioners' sugar (to thicken icing)
2 cups finely chopped almonds

Cream the butter and 1 cup of confectioners' sugar, then add the 4 egg yolks and the cream and stir well. Add in sifted flour and mix. Roll out dough on a surface lightly sprinkled with flour and confectioners' sugar until the dough is about ¼ inch thick. Cut into diamond shapes with a crinkle-edged pastry wheel and place on greased baking sheets. Bake at 350°F for about 15 minutes, then allow them to cool on the sheets.

While the cookies cool, you can prepare the icing. Beat the 2 remaining egg yolks with the water. Add in confectioners' sugar a little bit at a time, stirring, until you have a moderately thick paste. Ice the cookies liberally and then sprinkle on the almonds thickly. Return to the oven for 3 to 4 minutes to crisp.

YIELD: 3 dozen cookies

© Michael Grand

© John Pemberton

CHOCOLATE CHEESECAKE CHUNKS

THESE CREAMY MINI-CHEESECAKES SIT ATOP A MOUTH-watering chocolate nut crust — and they are surprisingly simple to make.

½ cup butter

1¼ cups chocolate wafer
     crumbs (about 30 wafers)

1 cup chopped nuts

2 packages (3 ounces each)
     cream cheese, softened

⅓ cup granulated sugar

⅓ cup unsweetened cocoa
     powder

1 egg

1 teaspoon vanilla

Preheat oven to 350°F. Melt butter in a 9-inch-square baking pan. Stir in crumbs and ½ cup nuts. Press to cover bottom of pan. In a small bowl, beat cream cheese, sugar, cocoa, egg, and vanilla at medium speed until smooth. Pour over crust and sprinkle with remaining ½ cup nuts. Bake 20 minutes. Let stand at room temperature 2 hours. Cut into 1-inch squares with a sharp knife. Store, covered, in refrigerator.

These cookies are best presented in a single layer on a large, round, flat tray or basket lined with colored cellophane or a doily. Cover with plastic wrap to keep cookies in place until delivery.

YIELD: 80 chunks

ALMOND CRESCENTS

T HESE BUTTERY, NUTTY DELIGHTS ARE EASY TO MAKE AND are best eaten soon after baking. The combination of almonds and chocolate glaze makes them a delicious, elegant cookie dessert.

1¼ cups (3½ sticks) butter
½ cup granulated sugar
1 teaspoon vanilla
4 cups all-purpose flour
1 cup chopped blanched almonds

GLAZE
½ cup semisweet chocolate bits
1 tablespoon butter

In a large bowl, beat butter, sugar, and vanilla until light and fluffy. Mix in flour and nuts and knead until smooth, about 5 minutes. Refrigerate for several hours. Preheat oven to 350°F. Roll one teaspoon of dough at a time in the palm of your hand until it is approximately 2½ inches long. Shape into a crescent. Space crescents about 1 inch apart on ungreased cookie sheets and bake for 8 minutes. Cool on racks.

To make the glaze, gently melt the chocolate and butter together in a double boiler over low heat. Let cool slightly. Dip one end of each crescent into the chocolate mixture until well coated.

YIELD: 5 dozen crescents

Southern Hospitality Lemon Bars

Celebrate New Years' Day with these lemon bars borrowed from Southern plantation soirees.

1 cup plus 2 tablespoons flour	1 cup sugar
½ cup butter, softened	Finely grated rind of 1 lemon
¼ cup plus 2 tablespoons confectioners' sugar	3-4 tablespoons lemon juice
2 eggs	½ teaspoon baking powder

Mix 1 cup flour, butter, and ¼ cup confectioners' sugar into a soft dough, and press evenly into the bottom of a 9-inch-square greased and floured baking pan. Bake on the middle rack of a 350°F oven for 20 minutes.

As this bakes, mix eggs, sugar, lemon rind, lemon juice, and 2 tablespoons flour. When crust is done, quickly whisk baking powder into the lemon mixture. Pour on the lemon topping, and bake for 25 more minutes. Let cool and dust with remaining confectioners' sugar.

Yield: 25 bars a little less than 2 inches square

DOUBLE CHOCOLATE BALLS

THESE SCRUMPTIOUS LITTLE COOKIES ARE A CHOCOLATE LOVER'S DELIGHT.

1 package (6 ounces) semisweet chocolate bits

3 tablespoons corn syrup

½ cup strong coffee

1 package (8 ounces) chocolate wafers, crushed

1 cup chopped nuts

½ cup confectioners' sugar

⅓ cup chopped candied red cherries

Granulated sugar

Gently melt chocolate in a double boiler over low heat. Remove from heat and stir in syrup and coffee; cool to room temperature. Meanwhile, in a large bowl, mix wafers, nuts, confectioners' sugar, and cherries. Add the chocolate mixture and stir to blend. Let stand for 30 minutes. Shape into 1-inch balls with fingers. Roll in granulated sugar, then refrigerate, covered, until ready to pack for gift-giving.

YIELD: 2 ½ dozen balls

© John Pemberton

© Jake Dombelton

PEANUT BUTTER BALLS

THESE CHEWY CHILL-AND-SERVE TREATS COMBINE THE RICH taste of peanut butter with the delicate sweetness of honey and coconut. And because they are easy to prepare and involve no work at the stove, these cookies are a great way to introduce a small child to cookie-making.

- 1 cup peanut butter
- ½ cup honey
- 1 cup quick oats
- 1 cup chopped, mixed dried fruit
- 1 cup shredded sweetened coconut

In a large bowl, combine all ingredients except coconut. Mix well with wooden spoon and shape into 1-inch balls. Roll balls in coconut. Serve immediately or chill.

YIELD: 4 dozen balls

© John Pemberton

Snowmen

THESE SNOWMEN ARE EVEN MORE FUN TO BUILD THAN THE usual kind — and are certainly tastier. Frost on the hats and mufflers, and do not forget the raisin eyes and buttons.

1 cup butter, softened
½ cup granulated sugar
1 teaspoon vanilla
2 cups all-purpose flour
Raisins, coarsely chopped
Chocolate chips
3 tablespoons confectioners' sugar

FROSTING

2½ cups confectioners' sugar
½ teaspoon cream of tartar
2 egg whites
8 drops food coloring of choice

Preheat oven to 325°F. In a large bowl, beat butter, sugar, and vanilla until light and fluffy. Stir in flour to blend well. For each snowman, shape dough into 3 balls, measuring 1 inch, ¾ inch, and ½ inch. Place on ungreased cookie sheets with the sides of the balls touching and press together gently; space snowmen about 1 inch apart. Insert raisins for eyes (and buttons, if desired). Bake 18 minutes. Cool on racks.

To prepare frosting, in a medium bowl, beat confectioners' sugar, cream of tartar, egg whites, and green food coloring at high speed until stiff. Fill pastry bag fitted with writing tip about one-third full with frosting. Decorate cookies with frosting and chips as shown in picture or as desired. Sprinkle lightly with confectioners' sugar.

YIELD: 2 dozen snowmen

Holiday Linzer Cookies

Traditional in Austria during the Christmas holidays, these cookies are often given to children on St. Nicholas Day in early December. Although they are tender, they will ship well if you make them small enough.

½ cup butter
⅓ cup sugar
1 egg
½ teaspoon vanilla
¼ teaspoon grated lemon rind

1 cup flour
¼ teaspoon salt
Granulated sugar
¼ cup raspberry or apricot jam

Cream together butter and sugar until light and fluffy, then add egg and vanilla. Stir rind, flour, and salt together, then add to the butter mixture. Wrap in waxed paper and chill 2 to 3 hours.

Pinch off a piece of dough and roll into a ball about 1 inch in diameter. Roll in granulated sugar, and place it on a greased and floured cookie sheet. Continue with the remaining dough, placing balls 2 inches apart. Bake for 5 minutes at 375°F.

With the back of a spoon, make an indentation in the top of each ball. Bake 8 more minutes, until the edges are slightly browned. Remove from the oven and spoon a small amount of jam into the indentations. Move to wire racks and let cool.

YIELD: 15 cookies

© Michael Grand

© Michael Grand

Chewy Peanut Cookies

THESE CHEWY COOKIES ARE DELICIOUS ANY SEASON, BUT they are particularly scrumptious when eaten as a snack with coffee while wrapping Christmas presents. Oat flour keeps them moist enough for gift boxes that have a long way to travel.

1 cup butter	1 teaspoon vanilla
1 cup smooth peanut butter	2¼ cups oat flour (see note)
½ cup sugar	2 teaspoons baking soda
1 cup packed brown sugar	¼ teaspoon salt
2 eggs	1 cup finely chopped peanuts

Beat together butter, peanut butter, and sugars, then mix in eggs and vanilla. Combine oat flour, baking soda, and salt, and mix into peanut butter mixture well. Stir in nuts. Wrap dough in waxed paper and chill about 1 hour.

Roll dough into 1-inch balls and place on ungreased baking sheets. Flatten each with the tines of a fork dipped in sugar to make a criss-cross pattern. Bake at 350°F for

10 minutes, until the edges are golden brown. Cool on sheets.

YIELD: 50 cookies

NOTE: To make oat flour, place 1 cup oatmeal in a blender or food processor. Blend about 1 minute at medium-high speed. Continue adding oatmeal a bit at a time until you have the correct amount of flour.

CHILDRENS' DELIGHT

THESE PEANUT BUTTER OATMEAL DROPS ARE TOPPED OFF with miniature mountains of chocolate kisses, incorporating just about everything a kid could want into one cookie. They require a few minutes at the stove, but no baking.

2 cups granulated sugar

¼ cup unsweetened cocoa powder

½ cup milk

½ cup butter

½ cup peanut butter

½ teaspoon vanilla

2½ cups quick oats

FROSTING

(see the frosting for snowmen cookies on page 35, but do not add food coloring)

Chocolate chips or chocolate kisses

In a saucepan, bring sugar, cocoa, milk, and butter to a boil, stirring. Cook 1 minute, then remove from heat. Add peanut butter and vanilla and mix well. Pour over the oats in a large bowl. Mix again, and drop by teaspoonfuls

43

onto a cookie sheet lined with waxed paper. Prepare frosting as directed in the recipe on page 35. Flatten slightly with fingers and decorate with frosting and a chocolate chip or chocolate kiss. Chill for 1 hour. Serve immediately or store, covered, in the refrigerator.

YIELD: 4 dozen

Chocolate Orange Cheer Cookies

Y OU MAY WANT TO PRESENT THESE RICH COOKIES, DIPPED in semisweet chocolate and nuts, in a heart-shaped box as though they are chocolate candies. You can even make them small enough to be placed in fluted paper candy cups.

2½ cups sifted flour
2 teaspoons baking powder
¼ teaspoon salt
1 cup margarine
½ cup sugar
¾ cup packed brown sugar
2 eggs, beaten
1½ tablespoons orange liqueur
1½ tablespoons orange peel

1 cup chopped toasted hazelnuts
2 cups semisweet chocolate chips

GLAZE
1 cup semisweet chocolate chips
½ cup chopped toasted hazelnuts

Sift flour, baking powder, and salt together, and set aside. Cream margarine, sugar, and brown sugar until

47

light and fluffy, then blend in eggs. Add sifted ingredients, liqueur, and peel, mixing thoroughly, then fold in nuts and chocolate chips.

Drop by teaspoonfuls onto ungreased baking sheets and bake at 325°F for about 20 minutes. Transfer to wire racks and cool completely.

While the cookies are cooling, make the glaze. Melt chocolate in the top of a double boiler over simmering water. Remove from heat and dip bottom of cookies in the chocolate glaze. Dip chocolate-coated bottoms in the chopped nuts, and replace on baking sheets. Chill until chocolate is firm.

YIELD: 48 cookies

GINGERBREAD PEOPLE

Gingerbread cookies are a great project for children because the dough is not sticky or difficult to handle. They are also delicious.

3½ cups all-purpose flour	¾ cup granulated sugar
1 teaspoon baking soda	1 egg
¼ teaspoon salt	¾ cup molasses
1½ teaspoons ground ginger	1 teaspoon grated lemon zest
1½ teaspoons ground cinnamon	**FROSTING**
1 teaspoon ground cloves	⅓ cup egg whites
½ cup butter, softened	3¾ cups confectioners' sugar

Blend flour with baking soda, salt, ginger, cinnamon, and cloves in a medium-size bowl. In a large bowl, beat butter and sugar at high speed until light and fluffy. Beat in egg, then molasses and lemon peel until well blended. With a wooden spoon, stir in flour mixture, then mix with the wooden spoon or knead with hands until smooth.

Divide dough into four parts, wrap each in plastic, and refrigerate overnight.

Preheat oven to 375°F and grease cookie sheets. Roll out one part of the dough at a time on a floured pastry cloth or board to ⅛ inch thick. Cut into gingerbread people with cookie cutters or with a floured knife and place on cookie sheets, spacing about 1 inch apart. If you plan to use the cookies as ornaments, take a sharp knife and make a small hole at the top of each cookie through which you can thread a ribbon. Bake 6 to 8 minutes or until lightly browned. Cool cookies on racks.

In the meantime, in a medium-size bowl at medium speed, beat egg whites and confectioners' sugar to make a smooth, stiff frosting — about 1 minute. Cover with a damp cloth until ready to use.

To decorate cookies, spoon frosting into a pastry bag fitted with the smallest round tip. Work with bag about one-third full. Pipe frosting along borders of cookies and within to form hair, features, and clothing of gingerbread people. Let frosting dry, then store in a covered bag.

YIELD: Approximately 2 dozen, depending on size

© John Pemberton

© John Pemberton

Speculaas

Kids will enjoy making these adorable teddy bear cookies. They can even be allowed to harden and then be hung on the Christmas tree.

3 cups all-purpose flour	1 cup butter, softened
1½ teaspoons ground cinnamon	1¼ cups light brown sugar, packed
1 teaspoon ground cloves	1 egg
1 teaspoon ground ginger	½ cup sliced bleached almonds
¼ teaspoon baking powder	
¼ teaspoon salt	

Blend flour with spices, baking powder, and salt in a medium-size bowl. In a large bowl, beat butter and sugar at high speed until light and fluffy. Beat egg in well. With a wooden spoon, stir in half the flour mixture, then add the remaining flour and almonds, mixing with a wooden spoon or kneading with hands. Divide dough into four parts, wrap in plastic, and refrigerate for several hours. (If you are using a mold, chill it as well.)

Preheat oven to 350°F and grease two cookie sheets. Remove one quarter of the dough from the refrigerator and flatten it with your hands. Oil your mold and lightly flour it. Using your fingers, press dough firmly into the mold. Trim any excess dough from the mold with a knife. Transfer the cookies onto greased cookie sheets with a spatula, spacing about 1 inch apart. Refrigerate dough trimmings to be rerolled later. Lightly flour—but do not re-oil—cookie mold. Repeat process with remaining dough. When cookie sheets are full, bake cookies for 20 to 25 minutes or until golden brown around the edges. Store in a covered tin.

YIELD: 2 dozen cookies

SUGAR COOKIES

WHATEVER THE SHAPE YOU WISH TO MAKE, YOU CAN find cookie cutters to match. These sugar cookies can be shaped as Christmas trees, Santas, snowmen, bells, or stars and then decorated with frosting in appropriate colors.

½ cup butter
¾ cup sugar
1 egg
½ teaspoon vanilla
1½ cups flour
¼ teaspoon salt

¼ teaspoon baking powder
1 tablespoon milk

FROSTING
(see the snowmen cookies
frosting on page 35, using
food color of choice)

Cream together butter and sugar until light and fluffy, then beat egg and vanilla in well. Sift together flour, salt, and baking powder, then mix them into the creamed mixture along with the milk. Wrap dough in waxed paper and chill for about an hour.

Roll out dough on a lightly floured surface until thin. Cut with cookie cutters or a knife into desired shapes, and transfer them to ungreased baking sheets. Bake at 375°F for about 8 minutes, until lightly golden around the edges (the thinner you roll the dough, the less time they will take to cook). Cool a moment on the sheets, then move to wire racks to cool completely.

Once cooled, you may decorate them with frosting (see page 35 for directions), in any way you wish.

YIELD: 30 cookies

Swiss Chalets

THESE FUN-TO-MAKE COOKIES CAN BE CUT INTO OTHER shapes using different cookie cutters. Adding food coloring to the frosting will open up even more possibilities.

2½ cups all-purpose flour

½ teaspoon baking soda

1 teaspoon baking powder

½ teaspoon salt

1½ teaspoons ground cinnamon

1 teaspoon ground ginger

½ teaspoon ground cloves

¼ teaspoon freshly grated nutmeg

½ cup butter, softened

½ cup granulated sugar

1 egg

½ cup molasses

FROSTING
(see the snowmen cookies frosting on page 35, you can leave out food coloring if desired)

Silver candy balls

Blend flour, baking soda, baking powder, salt, and spices in a medium-size bowl. In a large bowl, beat the butter and sugar at medium speed until light and fluffy. Beat in egg well, then beat in molasses. Stir in the flour mixture to blend well. Divide dough into three parts, wrap in plastic, and refrigerate 3 hours.

Preheat oven to 350°F. On a floured surface, roll out dough, one third at a time, to ⅛ inch thick. With a 2" x 1" house-shaped cookie cutter, cut out cookies and place on ungreased cookie sheets, about 1 inch apart. Bake 5 to 6 minutes. Cool on racks.

Make frosting as described on page 35, then spread on cookies (or pipe on using a pastry bag). Decorate as desired. Store in a covered tin.

YIELD: 3 dozen cookies

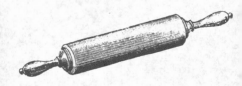

STAINED GLASS WINDOWS

C LEAR CANDIES MELTED INTO DIFFERENT SHAPES GIVE
  these cookies the look of stained glass. They are elegant decorations for either Christmas or Easter. Instead
of using cookie cutters, you can also create original cookie
designs by rolling the dough into long ropes and molding
them into different shapes.

1½ cups butter	1¼ teaspoons nutmeg
1⅓ cups sugar	5¼ cups flour
½ cup milk	Clear hard candies, sorted
4 eggs, well beaten	by color and then crushed

Cream together butter and sugar. Beat milk together
with eggs and add to butter mixture. Add nutmeg to flour,
and then mix gradually into butter mixture. Wrap in
waxed paper and chill for 1 hour.

Roll dough to ¼ inch thick and cut out with large
cookie cutters of your choice. From the center of each
cookie, cut out a circle or other shape using a smaller

cookie cutter. Be sure the edges remaining are at least ¼ inch wide. Place on a baking sheet that has been covered with foil. Fill the centers with crushed candy, one color to a hole. If you are using the cookies as ornaments, pass heavy white thread through the top of each cookie to form a loop.

Bake 6 to 9 minutes at 350°F or until candy melts. Cool 5 minutes to solidify candy before moving the cookies carefully to wire racks.

YIELD: 5 dozen cookies

Moravian White Christmas Cookies

These classic Moravian treats are a favorite in Bethlehem, Pennsylvania.

1½ cups butter, softened	½ teaspoon salt
3 cups confectioners' sugar	½ tablespoon nutmeg
4 eggs, well beaten	3 tablespoons sherry
4 cups flour, sifted	

Cream the butter and sugar, then add eggs. Sift together flour, salt, and nutmeg twice to lighten. Add sifted ingredients to butter mixture alternately with the sherry, stirring lightly. Wrap dough in waxed paper and refrigerate 6 hours to overnight.

Roll out chilled dough on a floured surface until very thin. Cut into shapes by hand or with cookie cutters. Place on ungreased baking sheets, and bake at 350°F until softly golden around the edges.

YIELD: 80 cookies

Cinnamon Stars

C HRISTMAS WOULDN'T BE CHRISTMAS IN SWEDEN WITH OUT these fine-textured cinnamon and almond meringues. If you put these in a box for shipping, wrap each one separately in white tissue paper.

3 egg whites at room temperature

Dash of salt

1¼ cups super-fine sugar

1 tablespoon cinnamon

5 cups almond meal (or 5½ cups finely ground unblanched almonds)

Beat egg whites and salt with an electric mixer until they form soft peaks. Slowly add the sugar, and beat for 10 minutes on high speed. Spoon out and set aside ¾ cup of the meringue. Slowly fold the cinnamon into the remaining meringue and beat the mixture for 15 seconds. Gently fold in 4 ½ cups of the almond meal, until well-incorporated. Sprinkle work surface with some of the spare meal, and pat or roll out dough to about ¼ inch, using more meal if needed to prevent sticking. Cut dough with a star-shaped cookie cutter. Place stars on greased and floured cookie sheets.

Spread a portion of the reserved meringue on top of each star, and set the cookies aside in a cool place for 2 hours.

Bake at 350°F until cookies are very lightly browned and tops are firm to a gentle touch—about 20 minutes. Cool a few minutes on the sheets, then transfer to wire racks to cool completely.

YIELD: 25 stars

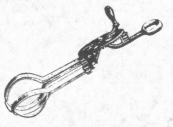

TWINKLES

For these double-decker delights you will need large and small star-shaped cookie cutters. To give them as gifts, place the cookies in a flat basket or tray lined with tissue paper in a single layer, lightly overlapping at the edges. Cover the basket with plastic wrap to keep the cookies in place.

2½ cups all-purpose flour	2 eggs
1 teaspoon baking powder	1 teaspoon vanilla
¼ teaspoon salt	6 tablespoons strawberry preserves
¾ cup butter, softened	
1 cup granulated sugar	

Blend flour, baking powder, and salt in a small bowl. In a large bowl, beat butter and sugar at medium speed until light and fluffy. Beat in eggs and vanilla well and then add to flour mixture. Divide dough into three parts, wrap in plastic, and refrigerate 3 hours.

Preheat oven to 350°F, and grease several cookie sheets. On a floured surface, roll one third of the dough at a time to ⅛ inch thick. Cut dough with a 2¾-inch star-shaped cookie cutter. With a 1¼-inch star-shaped cookie cutter, cut out the centers of half the larger stars. Place on a greased cookie sheet, spacing about 1 inch apart, and bake 6 to 8 minutes. Cool on racks.

Spread 1 teaspoon of preserves in the center of the star cookies without cutouts. Place a cookie with a cutout on top, lining up the stars' points on both cookies as shown in the photograph. Store in covered tins.

YIELD: 18 cookies

© John Pemberton

© John Pemberton

BUTTERFLIES

THESE LIGHT-AS-AIR CONFECTIONS ARE MADE WITH HOT butterfly-shaped cookie irons dipped into sweet batter. The cookie irons and holders are available at cookware stores.

2 eggs	½ teaspoon salt
2 teaspoons granulated sugar	1 tablespoon lemon extract
½ cup milk	Vegetable oil for deep frying
½ cup club soda	Confectioners' sugar
1 cup all-purpose flour	

Beat eggs lightly in a large bowl. Add sugar, milk, and club soda. In a separate bowl, blend flour and salt and add to egg mixture; beat until smooth. Beat in lemon extract. Fill a 5-quart frying pan or large pot with oil until two-thirds full. Heat oil to 400°F over medium-high heat. Dip cookie iron into hot oil; carefully remove and drain excess oil on paper towels. Then dip iron into the batter, covering iron almost to the top, and leave in for 3 seconds. Next, plunge the batter-covered iron into hot oil until lightly browned, about 1 minute. Ease butterfly off iron with fork and drain on paper towels. (Since the first few butterflies may stick to the iron, you may have to loosen them with a knife. As you continue to make them, they will come off more easily.) Sift confectioners' sugar over cookies when all are made. Serve immediately.

YIELD: 3 dozen cookies

Kringles

Firm, pretzel-shaped cookies, these hand-molded Danish treats take a little more time to make. But their delicious, buttery, not-too-sweet taste makes them well worth the effort.

¾ cup butter	2 cups all-purpose flour
½ cup granulated sugar	1 egg white beaten with 1 tablespoon water
3 hard-boiled egg yolks, sieved	¼ cup coarse sugar (or coarsely crushed sugar cubes)
1 raw egg	
½-¾ teaspoon ground cardamom	

Preheat oven to 375°F and grease several cookie sheets. In a medium-size bowl with a wooden spoon or electric mixer, beat butter, sugar, egg yolks, raw egg, and cardamom until light and fluffy. Stir in flour, mixing with hands until dough is stiff. Divide into four parts. Refrigerate, wrapped in plastic, for several hours. On floured surface, working with one part at a time, take a tablespoon of dough and roll into a 7-inch-long thin rope. Shape into a pretzel and place on a greased cookie sheet. Continue to make pretzels until dough is used up, spacing 2 inches apart on cookie sheets. Brush with beaten egg white, then sprinkle with coarse sugar. Bake 10 to 12 minutes until golden. Cool on racks and store in covered tin.

YIELD: About 2½ dozen

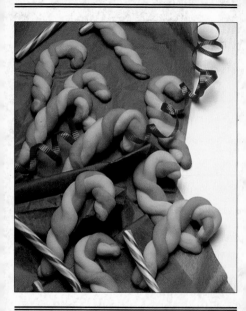

CANDY CANE COOKIES

THESE COLORFUL, FUN-TO-MAKE COOKIES TASTE OF MINT and are pretty enough to hang on the tree.

2½ cups all-purpose flour
½ teaspoon salt
1 cup butter, softened
1 cup confectioners' sugar
1 egg

1 teaspoon peppermint extract
1 teaspoon vanilla
Red food coloring

Preheat oven to 350°F. Blend flour and salt in a small bowl. In a large bowl, beat butter and sugar until light and fluffy. Beat in egg and extracts well, then stir in flour and salt. Divide dough in half and color one half with 8 drops red food coloring; refrigerate, wrapped in plastic, for 2 hours. Working with 1 teaspoon of dough at a time, form 5-inch-long, pencil-thin cylinders of each color. Twist one cylinder of each color together to look like a candy cane. Bake 12 to 15 minutes. Cool on racks.

YIELD: About 4 dozen

POLAR BEAR CLAWS

TENDER AND BUTTERY, THESE COOKIES ARE ELEGANT enough for the fanciest holiday cookie plate. To make a lovely assortment, present them with dark chocolate-covered shortbread.

1 cup butter, softened	4 ounces ground almonds
¾ cup granulated sugar	¼ teaspoon cloves
2½ cups flour	Confectioners' sugar

Cream together butter and sugar, then stir in flour, almonds, and cloves. Wrap dough in waxed paper, and chill at least 1 hour. Butter 6 madeleine pans thoroughly. Press 2 tablespoons of dough into each form.

Bake at 350°F for 15 to 20 minutes, until nicely browned. Turn out hot cookies onto a board sprinkled with confectioners' sugar, and dust the tops as well. Cool on the board.

YIELD: 48 cookies

© John Pemberton

PINWHEELS

T HE STREAK OF CHOCOLATE SPIRALING OUT FROM THE CEN-
ter of these cookies makes them extra special. The
dough can be prepared ahead of time and refrigerated;
then simply slice and bake.

½ cup butter, softened	¼ teaspoon salt
1 cup granulated sugar	1½ teaspoons baking powder
1 egg	1 ounce unsweetened
1 teaspoon vanilla	chocolate, melted
1¼ cups all-purpose flour	

In a large bowl, beat butter at medium speed until
light and fluffy. Gradually add sugar, egg, and vanilla
while continuing to beat. Sift flour into small bowl with
salt and baking powder and add to butter mixture. Mix
well. Divide dough in half and mix chocolate into one half.
Wrap both halves in plastic and refrigerate for several
hours.

Roll out plain and chocolate dough separately into oblongs about ⅛ inch thick. Place dark dough on top of light dough and roll up layers together, jelly-roll fashion. Wrap and refrigerate again overnight.

Preheat oven to 400°F, and grease several cookie sheets. Cut roll into ⅛-inch-thick slices and place on greased cookie sheets, spacing about 1 inch apart. Bake 8 minutes. Cool on racks.

YIELD: 3 dozen cookies

POINSETTIAS

T HESE COOKIES ARE EXTREMELY DELICATE. So IF YOU PLAN
to give them as a gift, be sure to pack them carefully
in a single layer in a flat basket or on a tray lined with
tissue paper. Tie the basket or tray with a ribbon and you
have a lovely and festive gift.

2½ cups all-purpose flour	1 teaspoon almond extract
¾ teaspoon salt	1 teaspoon vanilla
1 cup butter, softened	Red decorating sugar
1 cup confectioners' sugar	Silver candy balls
1 egg	

Blend flour and salt in a small bowl. In a medium
bowl, beat butter and sugar until light and fluffy. Beat in
egg, almond extract, and vanilla well. Stir in flour and mix
well. Divide dough into fourths, wrap in plastic, and
refrigerate overnight.

Preheat oven to 350°F and grease several cookie
sheets. On a floured surface, roll out one fourth of the

dough at a time to ⅛ inch thick. Cut into 2-inch squares. Working with one square at a time, make a ¾-inch cut from each corner running diagonally toward the center. Fold in alternate corners toward center of cookie (as in photograph), creating a pinwheel effect. Place on greased cookie sheets, spacing about 1 inch apart. Repeat with remaining dough.

Sprinkle center of each cookie with red sugar and place a silver candy ball in the middle. Bake 8 to 10 minutes. Cool on racks.

YIELD: 3½ dozen cookies

© John Pemberton

© John Pemberton

Sugar Santas

T HESE SANTA COOKIES ARE SURE TO PLEASE ANY CHILD
during the holiday season.

2½ cups all-purpose flour
1 teaspoon baking powder
½ teaspoon salt
¾ cup butter, softened
⅔ cup sugar
2 eggs

1 teaspoon vanilla
2 tablespoons milk

FROSTING
(see the snowmen cookies
frosting on page 35)

Blend flour, baking powder, and salt in a medium-size
bowl. In a large bowl, beat butter and sugar until fluffy.
Beat in eggs and vanilla well, then beat in milk. Stir in
flour mixture to blend well. Divide dough into three parts,
wrap in plastic, and refrigerate overnight.

Preheat oven to 350°F and grease several cookie
sheets. On a floured surface, roll dough, one part at a time,
to ⅛-inch thickness. Cut into 3-inch rounds and place

about 1 inch apart on cookie sheets. Bake 12 minutes or until lightly browned. Cool on racks.

In the meantime, prepare the frosting as directed on page 35 using red food coloring. To decorate cookies, fill a pastry bag fitted with a small decorative tip one-third full with frosting. Pipe on frosting for features.

YIELD: 3 dozen cookies

CRANBERRY BOGGERS

THESE DELICIOUS COOKIES ARE PERFECT FOR A THANKS-
giving or Christmas treat. The fruit keeps them moist.

3 cups cranberries	1 cup packed brown sugar
3 cups flour	1 egg
¼ teaspoon baking soda	¼ cup milk
1 teaspoon baking powder	2 tablespoons lemon juice
½ teaspoon salt	1 cup coarsely chopped
½ cup butter	walnuts
1 cup sugar	

Steam the cranberries 5 minutes and chop coarsely.
Sift flour, baking soda, baking powder, and salt together.
Cream butter and sugars until they are light and fluffy,
then beat in egg, milk, and lemon juice. Stir in the flour
mixture bit by bit. Add the cranberries and nuts. The
cranberries will be soft and will create a marbleized pattern in the dough. Drop by teaspoonfuls onto greased
cookie sheets, leaving about 1 inch between for spreading.

Bake at 375°F for about 15 minutes, until firm and golden. Transfer to racks to cool.

YIELD: Makes about 90 cookies.

OLD MAINE LACE COOKIES

THESE HOMEY SPICE COOKIES ARE A FAVORITE IN NEW England as soon as the snow starts falling. Make plenty for Thanksgiving nibbling and hide some away for Christmas — they'll keep.

¾ cup melted margarine	½ teaspoon salt
1 cup sugar	1 teaspoon cloves
¼ cup molasses	1 teaspoon cinnamon
1 egg	½ teaspoon ginger
2 cups flour	Granulated sugar
3 teaspoons baking soda	

In a mixing bowl, cream together the margarine, sugar, molasses, and egg. Sift together the flour, baking soda, salt, and spices, and stir them into the creamed mixture. Place in refrigerator for ½ hour to cool dough.

Scoop dough up by the teaspoonful, roll into little balls, and roll the balls in granulated sugar. Place them on greased baking sheets 2 inches apart to accommodate spreading. Bake at 350°F for 12 minutes, or until cookies are flat. Allow to cool for 5 minutes before removing them from the sheets.

Yield: 3 dozen cookies